Contents

Garden nature

You can spot all kinds of amazing wildlife everywhere you go. Sometimes you do not even need to go far! From bumblebees buzzing around your garden flowers to tall trees with beautiful cones and leaves, wildlife is everywhere, even on your very own doorstep!

In this book you will find 35 common garden wildlife creatures and plants to colour in as well as beautiful illustrations to copy, fantastic wildlife facts and even a spotter's guide so you can tick off what you've seen!

# Ladybird

This is a seven-spot ladybird.
It is bright red with black spots. Some ladybirds are yellow and black!

Bumblebee

Bumblebees buzz around flowers looking for nectar. They have bright stripes.

Wasp

You usually only see a common wasp in the summer. Watch out for its sting!

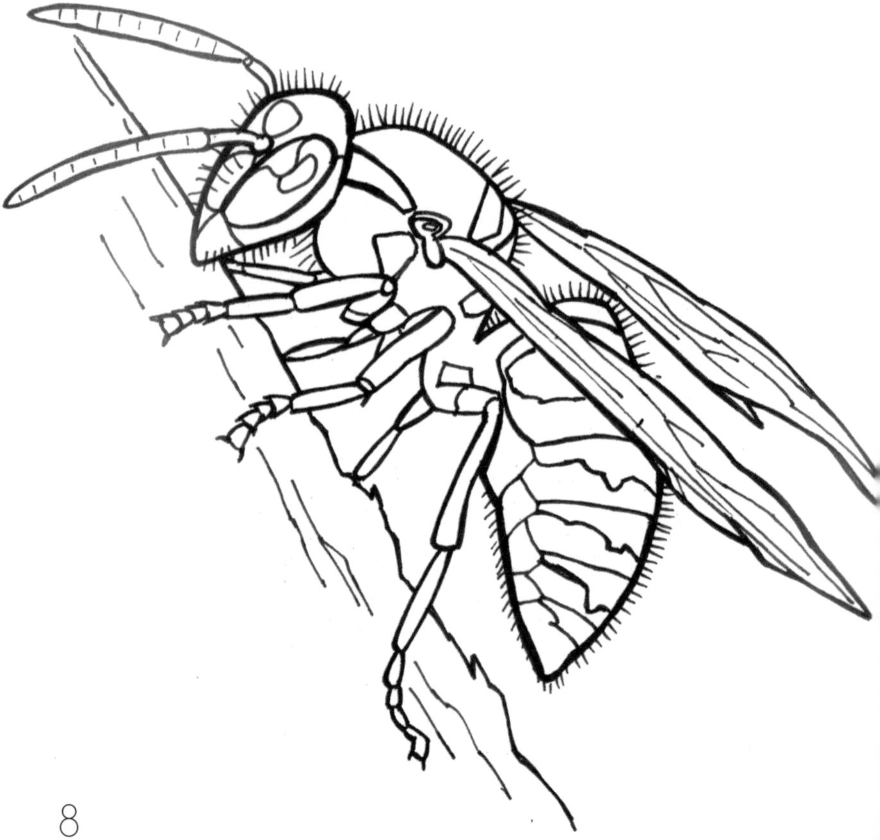

Bluebottle

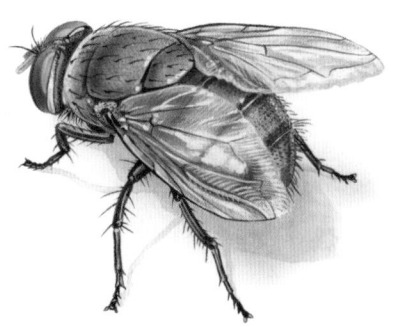

Shiny bluebottles are often spotted inside houses! They are hairy.

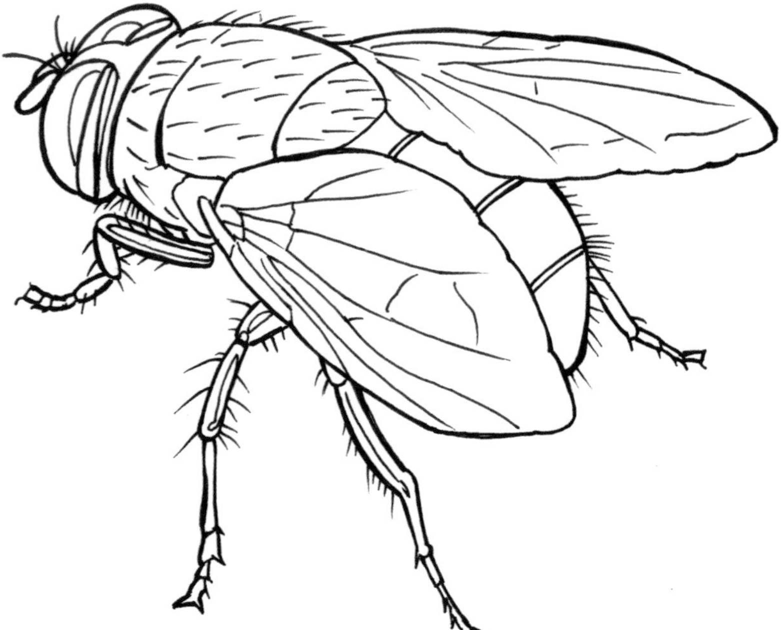

9

# Garden spider

Can you see
the cross of
white spots on
this large garden
spider's back?

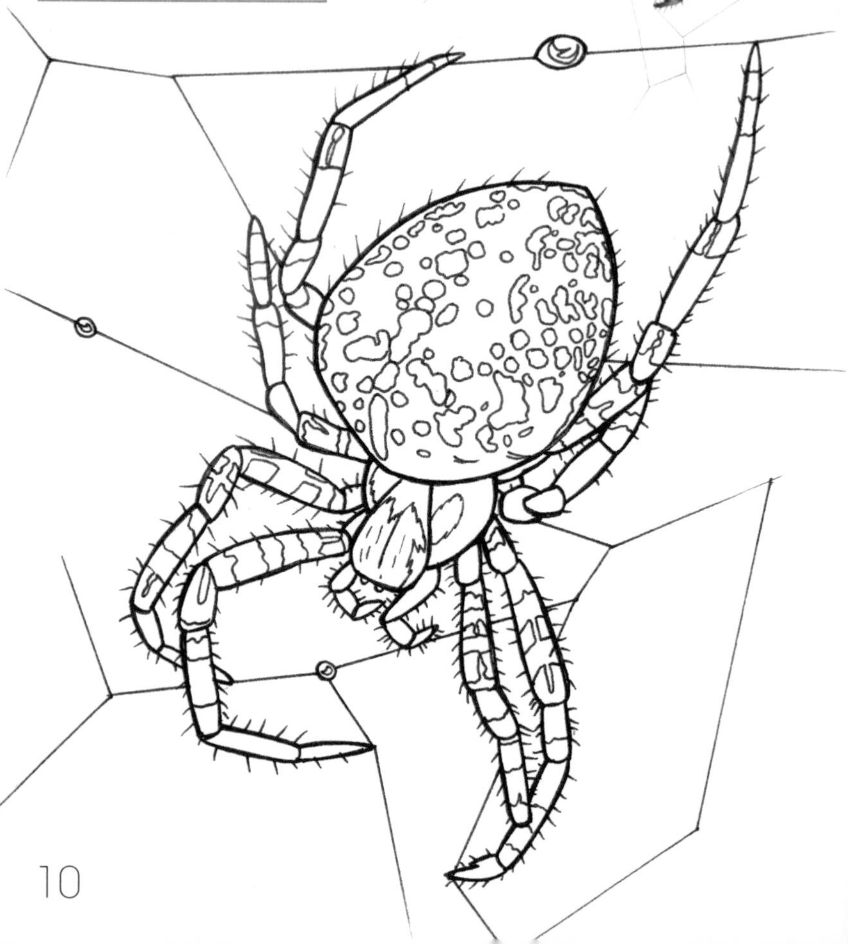

Green shield bug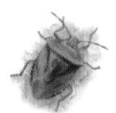

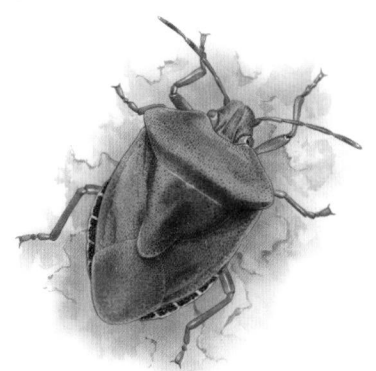

This bright green
insect is shaped
like a shield.
In winter it
turns brown!

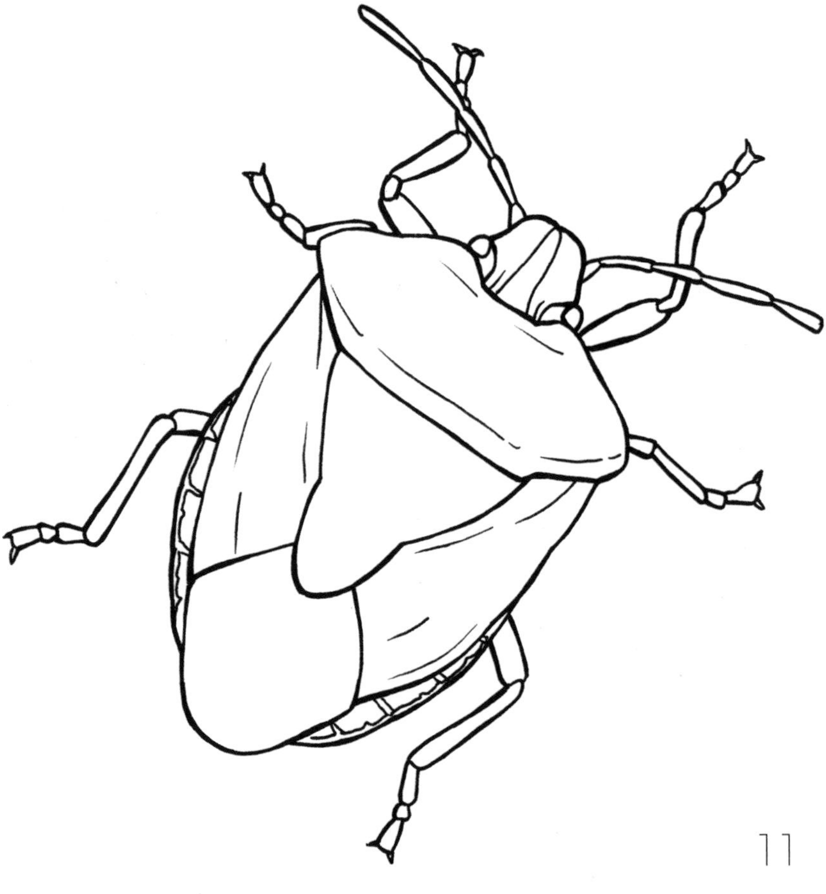

 # Garden snail

This common garden snail comes out in the rain. Look for its eyes at the end of its feelers.

Woodlouse

You'll often spot a woodlouse under a garden stone or log. Woodlice scurry about on their 14 legs.

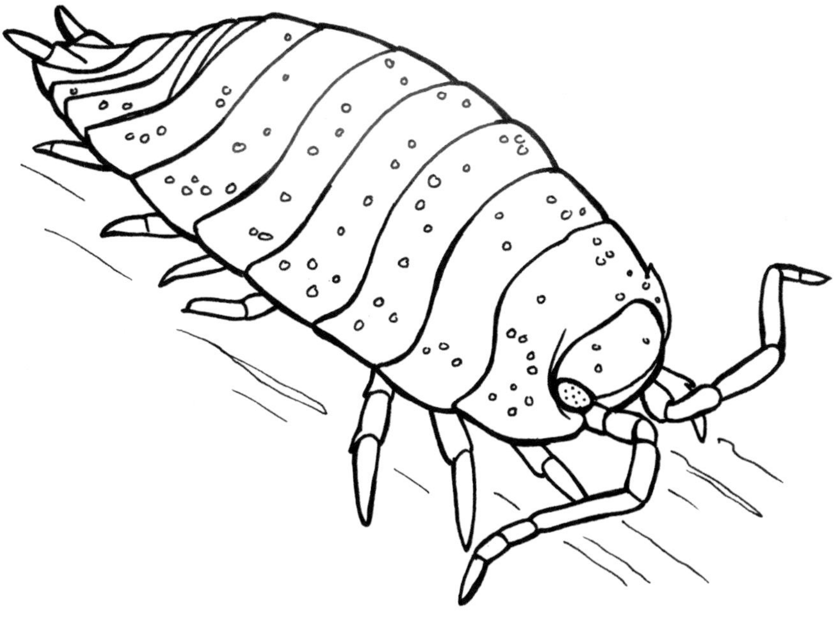

Common field grasshopper

This common field grasshopper is mostly green. But some are brown, pink, grey, black and even purple!

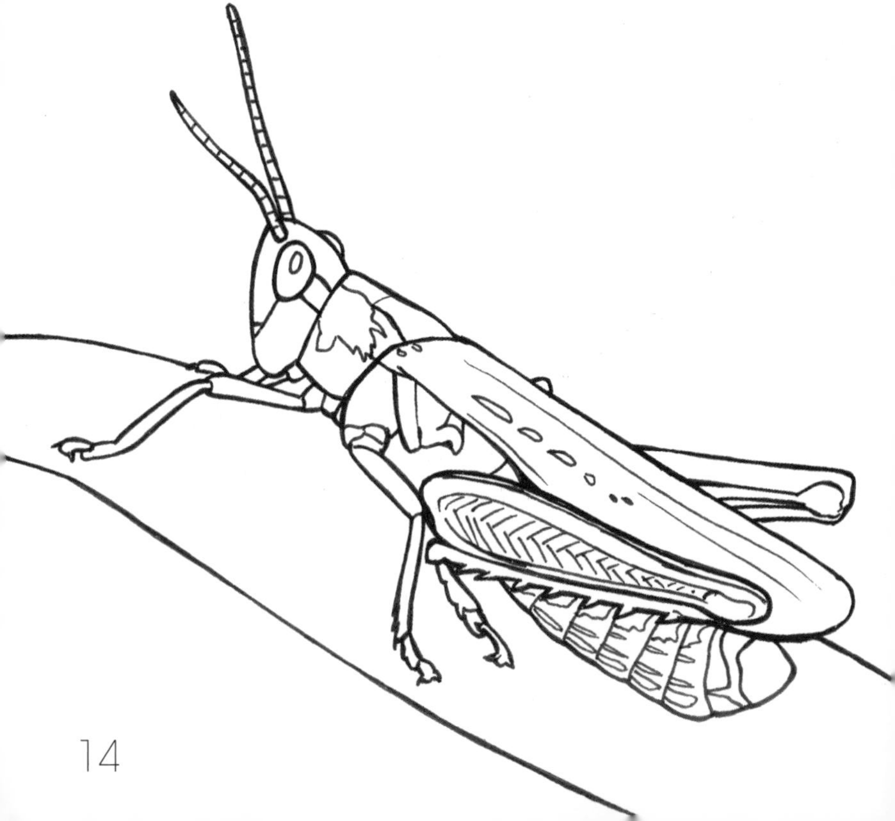

Badger

This mammal comes out at night looking for food to eat. It uses its big claws to dig for worms.

# Hedgehog

This garden creature has a furry face but all those prickly spikes could make it tricky to colour in!

Red fox

These night-time mammals sometimes have a white tip on the end of their tail.

# Mole

It's hard to see moles because they are usually underground. If you do spot one can you see its tiny eyes?

Grey squirrel

Look out for the long bushy tail of a grey squirrel in your garden. Red squirrels are much rarer.

House mouse

This mouse likes to live in your house! But look out for it in hedges too.

Pipistrelle bat

The pipistrelle
is a tiny bat.
When it closes
its wings it can fit
into a matchbox.

Common frog

These green and brown amphibians catch food with their sticky tongues.

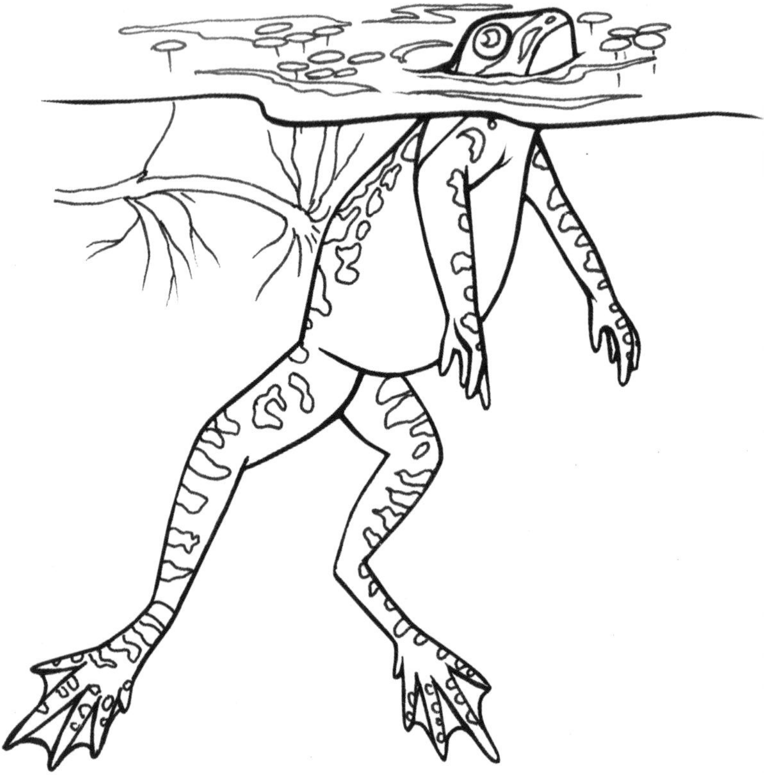

Foxglove

These tall flowers come in pink and white. They have dark spots on the inside of their petals.

 Primrose

Primroses have bright yellow flowers. Look for them from March to June.

Common poppy

These bright red flowers have four petals. The seed shakers on the end of the stems appear when the petals fall off.

# Holly

The green leaves
and red berries
on this tree are
often seen on
Christmas cards!

Brimstone butterfly

This bright yellow butterfly is said to be the colour of butter. Female brimstones have pale green wings instead of yellow.

Holly blue butterfly

Holly blue
caterpillars eat
holly leaves.
Later in the year,
they eat ivy.

Small tortoiseshell butterfly

This colourful butterfly travels a lot! Can you see the bright blue spots near the edges of its wings?

Painted lady butterfly

This bright
butterfly travels
all the way
from Africa! It's
supposed to look
like a lady wearing
lots of make-up.

30

Robin

This bird has
an orange face
and chest.
Look out for it
in your garden!

31

Blue tit

This bright blue
and yellow bird
can hang upside
down when it
is feeding!

Magpie

Magpies usually look black and white. But sometimes their dark feathers can look blue or green.

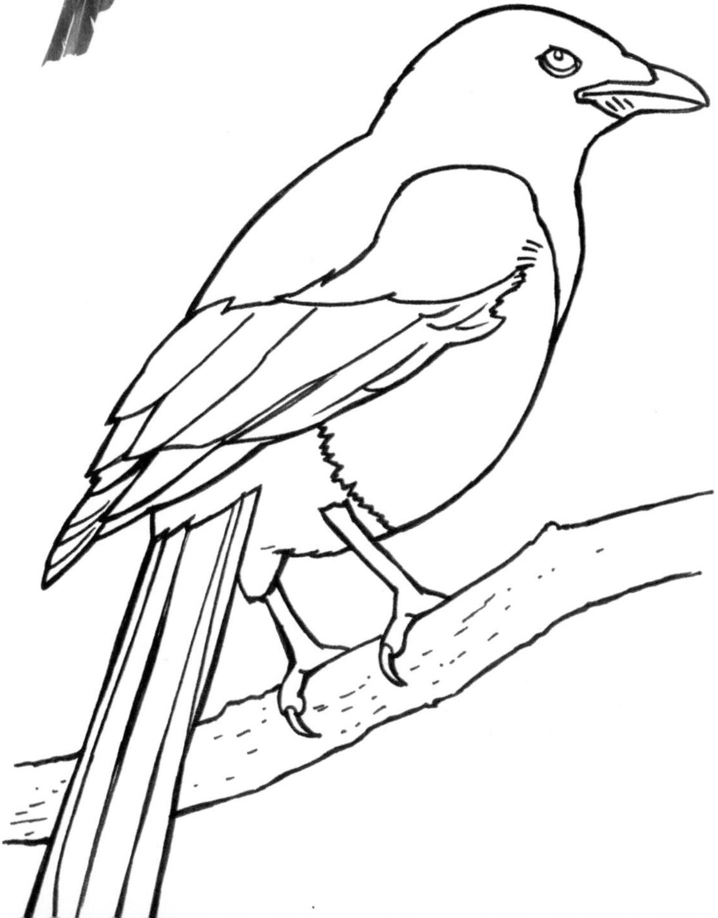

# House sparrow

The male house sparrow is more colourful than the female. Females have a brown head with no markings.

Woodpigeon

Look out for the woodpigeon's shiny purple and green neck with a white patch underneath.

Greenfinch

This mostly green bird has patches of yellow on its wings and its tail, and black on its tail and wings.

Chaffinch

This brightly coloured bird is a male. The females are mostly brown, instead of pink.

Wren

Wrens are tiny!
They have short
rounded wings
and weigh less
than a pencil.

38

Jay

This colourful bird can be spotted in woods. This jay has an acorn in its mouth.

Blackbird

Although the male blackbird is mostly black, watch out for the females which are brown.

Spotter's guide

How many of these things have you seen in your garden or out and about? Tick them when you spot them.

Ladybird
page 6

Bumblebee
page 7

Wasp
page 8

Bluebottle
page 9

Garden spider
page 10

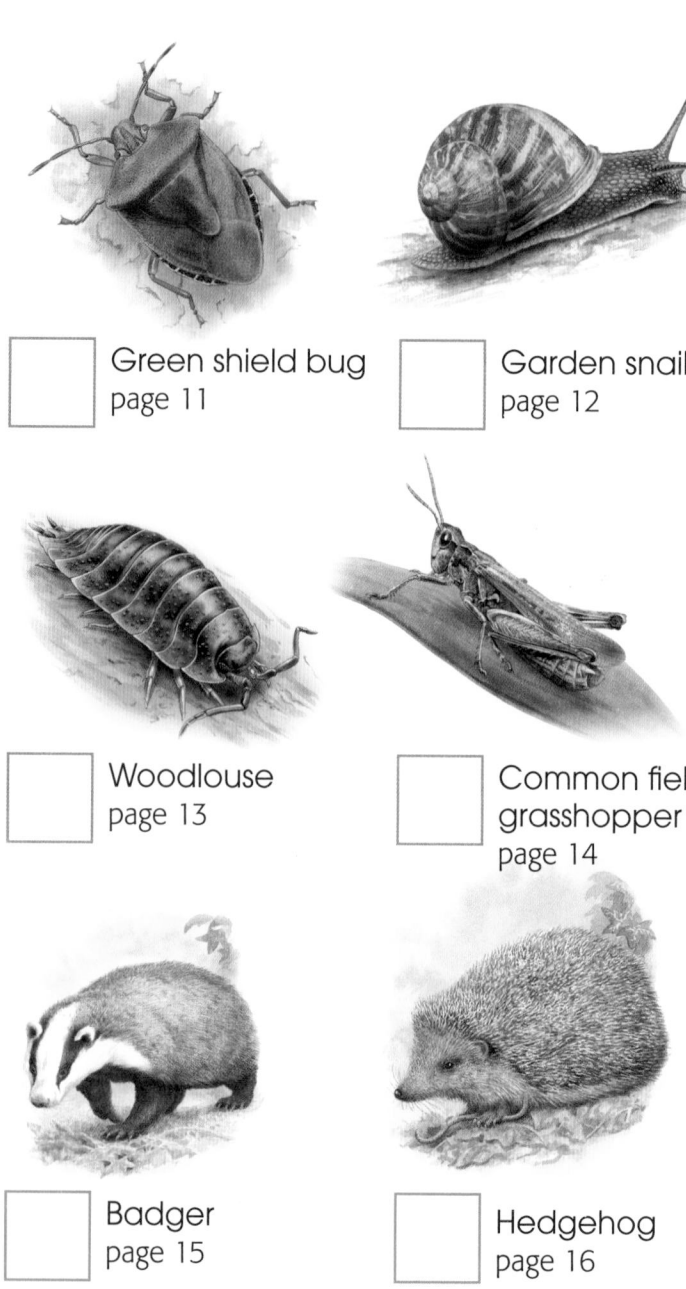

	Green shield bug page 11		Garden snail page 12
	Woodlouse page 13		Common field grasshopper page 14
	Badger page 15		Hedgehog page 16

Red fox
page 17

Mole
page 18

Grey squirrel
page 19

House mouse
page 20

Pipistrelle bat
page 21

Common frog
page 22

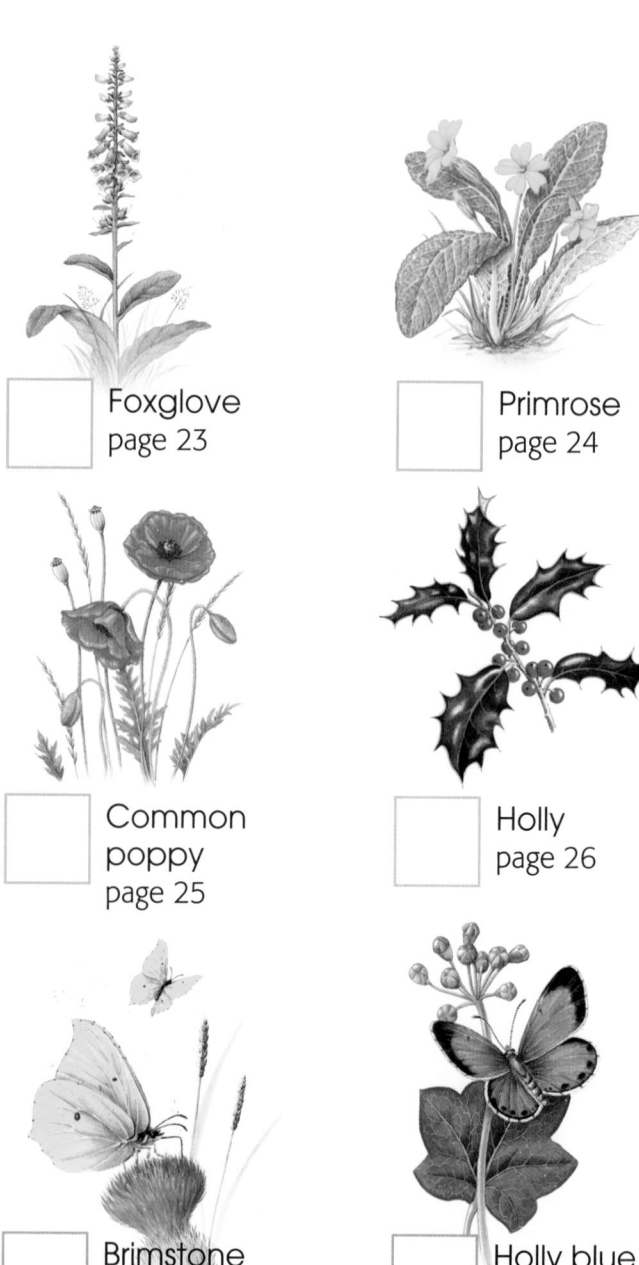

Foxglove
page 23

Primrose
page 24

Common
poppy
page 25

Holly
page 26

Brimstone
butterfly
page 27

Holly blue
butterfly
page 28

Small tortoiseshell butterfly
page 29

Painted lady butterfly
page 30

Robin
page 31

Blue tit
page 32

Magpie
page 33

House sparrow
page 34

Woodpigeon
page 35

Greenfinch
page 36

Chaffinch
page 37

Wren
page 38

Jay
page 39

Blackbird
page 40

Find out more

If you have enjoyed this colouring book and would like to find out more about garden wildlife you might like RSPB Wildlife Explorers.

Visit www.rspb.org.uk/youth to find lots of things to make and do, and to play brilliant wildlife games.

If you like learning about nature you might also like this RSPB book:

HB 978-1-4081-7888-1
PB 978-1-4081-7889-8

RSPB
a million voices for nature

The RSPB Bumper Book of Wildlife Stories

Pat Kelleher
Stories illustrated by Daniel Howarth